EMS BY KEVIN BOWEN

PLAYING BASKETBALL
with the VIET CONG

KEVIN BOWEN

Playing Basketball
with
the Viet Cong

CURBSTONE PRESS

FIRST EDITION, 1994
Copyright 1994 by Kevin Bowen
ALL RIGHTS RESERVED

Printed in the U.S. on acid-free paper by BookCrafters
cover design: Les Kanturek

Curbstone Press is a 501(c)(3) nonprofit publishing house whose operations are supported in part by private donations and by grants from ADCO Foundation, J. Walton Bissell Foundation, Inc., Witter Bynner Foundation for Poetry, Inc., Connecticut Commission on the Arts, Connecticut Arts Endowment Fund, Lannan Foundation, LEF Foundation, Lila Wallace-Reader's Digest Literary Publishers Marketing Development Program, administered by the Council of Literary Magazines and Presses, The Andrew W. Mellon Foundation, National Endowment for the Arts, and The Plumsock Fund.

Library of Congress Cataloging-in-Publication Data

Bowen, Kevin, 1947-
       Playing basketball with the Viet Cong : poems / by Kevin Bowen.—
   1st ed.
           p.   cm.
       ISBN: 1-880684-20-9 (pa) : $10.95
       1. Vietnamese Conflict, 1961-1975—Poetry.   2. Soldiers' writings,
   American.   3. War poetry, American.   I. Title.
   PS3552.0862P57   1994
   811'.54—dc20   94-30715

distributed by
InBook
Box 120261
East Haven, CT 06512

published by
CURBSTONE PRESS
321 Jackson Street
Willimantic, CT 06226

For Leslie

CONTENTS

Introduction

What the poem translates, I propose we call experience, on condition that
this word be taken literally—from Latin, *experiri:* the risky crossing...
—Phillipe Lacoue-Labarthe

In August, 1968, Kevin Bowen was sent to Vietnam to serve with the First
Air Cavalry Division in Quang Tri Province near the DMZ and in Tay Ninh
Province on the Cambodian Border. He was twenty-one years old, and
having found college irrelevant to the exigencies of conscience, had
positioned himself for conscription. A working-class son of the Catholic
Worker movement, he remembers the hubris of his assumptions regarding
social change, and a certain guilt: if he didn't go to war, who would go in
his place? What would happen to the soldier who stood *for* him on the field
of battle?

This deeply altruistic and ethical self-interrogation continued after the
war, when he returned to the university, studying literature, unloading
freight trucks at night and selling fruit on weekends. When the Paris Peace
Talks were underway in the summer of 1971, he took his fruit money and
went to Paris to stand outside the talks as the political future of Vietnam
and the moral future of the United States was determined. From France, he
traveled to Spain and Italy, wondering if it were possible to write poetry
after Vietnam, echoing Theodor Adorno's fear that, after Auschwitz, all
documents of civilization become documents of barbarity. The poet Edmund
Jabès, himself a war refugee, answered "I say that we must write. But we
cannot write as before," and it is an answer Bowen echoes, with the
publication of this first book of poems, *Playing Basketball with the Viet
Cong.*

Just as its title reinscribes the humanity of a former enemy, this book
writes its way through cratered memory, turning the still-contaminated
ground, the alluvium studded with war's still-exploding ordnance,
excavating the site of historical and personal trauma.

"Writing," says Claire Nouvet, "leaves the trace of an original disaster
which was not experienced in the first person precisely since it ruined this
first person, reduced it to a ghostlike status, to being a 'me without me.'" In
Bowen's work, language is the revenant, and hope an *unharvested field.* The
allegorical palace of the star-crossed marriage of north and south that
begins this collection is itself chimerical, contingent on the perceptions of
disbelieving armies, and throughout the work, specters continue their

procession: the soul's *surplice / trailing the jungle floor*, a soldier dancing *in trails of smoke above my head, the names, the eyes / ...staring in at the door, ghosts passing over a river*, then what the poet's sleeping wife sees: *a figure in black, arm draped / across my shoulder, as if to protect me*—in a country of ancestral worship, a sustained proliferation of the dead. As Vietnam is haunted, so is the soldier, his language, and the souls of his compatriots. In Bowen's work, the war becomes readable, across the scarred map of the abandoned war zone, and the blank page anticipating the poem. Bowen writes *on the war's terms* and the war denies any other way of writing. The poet reads his present life through the scrim of his past. In the poem "Incoming" he recounts the emotional effect of witnessing wounded comrades under a mortar attack, then transposes his consciousness onto a shopping mall:

> In a moment, it's over.
> But it takes a lifetime to recover,
> let out the last breath
> you took as you dove.
> This is why you'll see them sometimes,
> in malls, men and women off in corners:
> the ways they stare through the windows in silence.

"What we have seen with our own eyes, what we have personally experienced, what we were and what we did," wrote Paul Valéry, "—these should provide us with the questionnaire, drawn from our own life; we shall then ask history to fill it out, and she must do her best to answer when we ask her about times we never lived through. What was it like to live in such and such a period?" Bowen tells us that *evenings smell of kerosene and coal, sampans* become *red notes on a green bannered sea*, that the gunfire was so heavy that *he still wears it like a shirt*, that *the secret is not to panic*. This is not the Vietnam we knew from memories of combat, nor from television broadcasts, nor from a granite wall of names, but the Vietnam that invented us, who live in its aftermath. From the title poem:

> You never thought then
> that this grey-haired man in sandals
> smoking Gauloises on your back porch,
> drinking your beer, his rough cough
> punctuating tales of how he fooled
> the French in '54
> would arrive at your back door
> to call you out to shoot baskets.

Bowen's work is a poetry of witness, marked by its passage through extremity, itself constituting evidence of the war, but moving beyond the conventions of "war poetry," even those established since World War I. The soldier poet writes through and beyond the combat zone and returns to it, years later and repeatedly, so as to prevent the stasis of memorialization, opening the wound long enough to begin a just and genuine reconciliation. This is arduous work, less for the faint-hearted than the experience of war itself:

> One day he walks
> straight off the earth,
> right into the brown, wrinkled
> hide of an elephant,
> carves meat for a starving platoon,
> takes machete and scalpel,
> makes cut after cut
> until he's covered
> in blood and muscle,
> fighting for air.

The past is *a woodcut on rice paper / Two women in conical hats / load rocks along a road. / In the background, trucks / grow wings of camouflage.* These are the harsh brush-strokes of a shared history. The Viet Cong have come as guests to the poet's Boston house, where they will take over his kitchen to prepare a feast of delicacies for American combat veterans, and later play basketball. Nothing like this has been written out of war. Kevin Bowen has heeded Rainer Marie Rilke's advice: "To hold our innermost conscience alert, which with every fully formed experience tells us whether it is thus, as it now stands, altogether to be answered for in its truthfulness and integrity: *that* is the foundation of every artistic production, which ought to be laid even there where an inspiration kept in suspense can, so to speak, do without the ground." The *innermost conscience* that first compelled Kevin Bowen to war has guided him through the realization of an extraordinary work.

Carolyn Forchè
August 17, 1994

Nhất Dạ Trạch: One Night Swamp

That night the Princess Tiên Dung
strolled out along the canals
that lined the broad Hong plain,
the world still held promise
and wonder for one so young.

The princess
was not surprised then
to meet the naked boy, Chứ Đồng Tứ,
parading under the Southern Cross.

And when,
against all proscriptions,
they married, and the king's soldiers
searched for their outlawed palace by the sea,
Tiên Dung could quietly wait the gods' further elaborations.

Too bad for the disbelieving armies.
Late that summer when they arrived
they found the palace gone, only a vast
impenetrable swamp, sea beasts surrounding their boats,
strange birds hovering overhead.

"If there's a heart, it's enough."
Phạm Tiến Duật, "Drivers of Lorries Without Windscreens"

First Casualty

They carried him slowly
down the hill.
One hand hung,
grey and freckled.
No one spoke but
stared straight up.
His body, heavy,
rolled back and forth
on the litter.
At LZ Sharon cooks spooned
the last hot food.
One by one the squad
walked back up hill.
"Don't mean nothing,"
someone said.
But all that winter
and into spring
I swear he followed us,
his soul, a surplice
trailing the jungle floor.

Cities of Dust

The click of footsteps down the hall,
high spiked heels on marble.
The shower running in the room next door.
Four a.m. The first night you never sleep,
air thick with gas and dust, flames
from street stalls, satay burning and sex
on stage and in back-street rooms.
The traffic could bury you here, mad orchestra of horns,
trucks, cars, motorcycles, the old elephant transport
reduced to bright colors of tuk tuks.
The unexpected always coming head on.
A barker on the street unfolds his wallet,
three naked girls leer from a white tub.
Their poses, the distraught angles, mimic postures
of dancers carved on sandstone temples an hour's drive away.
Turn and he's gone. Only traffic, the click of heels
(you know the sound), a life disappearing in dust and haze.

War Story for Paul

Let me tell it for you.
This time we'll try to get it right.
You're in the mountains,
come to a meadow.
You hesitate, you've seen it all
before, but decide to take the risk.
You take the first step out into the clearing,
and there they are,
twenty, maybe more,
their leader, the largest, in front.
He raises his fist.
Him first, then all of them,
the whole troop of rock apes,
beat the ground with two-foot clubs,
their eyes burn straight through you.
A mistake. You try to run,
but your legs won't budge.
Then suddenly they break free
and you're running down a trail,
but too soon it becomes the trail
of another story and a wooded ridge
above a river where you raise the wounded
into the liftship again. Each body
oozes white pus
you can't get off,
no matter how you try.
You run down the hill to the river,
roll in the sand hoping to beat
the flies and the smell and scum away,

but can't until you've torn every bit
of clothing off and run
naked in the stream toward me.

Rappelling

Camp Evans, 1968

We dive happily.
No good-byes,
one last look at the sergeant
and then over the edge
of the tower,
down ropes burning fast
through hooks.
The secret, not to panic,
to give in to desire
to clutch the line connects
the world above
to the one below
and so smash head first
against the wooden piles.
After the first fear,
there is calm
floating down,
hit the ground
run backwards tiptoe,
untangle the line for the next boy
and the next,
now descending all
four sides of the tower,
whirling like stars
out into the jungle.

Made in Hà Nội

for the disabled workers of An Dương

They live in different light,
fierce and burning.
At mid-day in shops
their shadows pose
against mud and amber walls,
kneel hooking rugs,
bend over sputtering machines
that spit cast-iron nails
and at long tables stretching latex patterns
for ping pong paddles,
"Made in Hà Nội."
Outside, day sings in the whirr
of bicycles, ring
of chimes and clack of drums
blowing up from West Lake temples.
Evenings, smells of kerosene and coal.
Lamps make shadows
charge in and out across the road.
Cycloes wait in empty lanes, at road stands,
poised to draw passers-by to fires.
Before the failing light
lovers hurry back from fields.

Ferry Crossing North of Hải Phòng

"a traveller's heart is rinsed in fresh waters."

Li Po

Up and down the coast
sampans sit becalmed,
red notes on a green-bannered sea.
Sounds of banging tin drums
drift down river,
mix with calls of women
hanging wash from fishing boats.
At the crossing, two trucks
overloaded with coal from the northern ranges
have driven the ferry aground
twenty yards from shore.
Children from fields,
feet caked with paddy mud,
cut back and forth across dikes.
Passengers throng the road
that runs out to greet them
lined with coconuts, oranges,
sweet bananas, loaves of bread.

At the water's edge an old man
stacks green bottles in rows
until they rise in entreaty.
Children stretch under trucks,
gather coal dust
to mix with dung
women carve in wheels by the road.
Nothing is wasted.

By the checkpoint, a crone
sings an old folk song,
but keeps losing the words.
She has no destination but crossing
back and forth,
each time she says, to die.
Thirty yards away, the captain
tries to guide the ferry to shore.
He runs from bow to bridge,
checking depth,
the engine's temper. He backs off
the bank, he assembles
the passengers in the stern.
The boat floats free.
Chains grind, tug
tightens to barge,
a faded wash of blue
uniforms, eyes
pleading for rescue
as he hits the throttle
and the engine stalls.
The ferry drifts into swells,
currents circling out to sea.
From shore, passengers
watch a second tug
cut loose its cargo,
nose into the river
downstream. Two boats
maneuver against mountains,
river and sky.
This time the weight of the second tug
sends the barge to land.
Bikes and trucks and people

merge, push off, then part,
each to their destinations.
River and road break free.

Incoming

Don't let them kid you —
The mind no fool like the movies,
doesn't wait for flash or screech,
but moves of its own accord,
even hears the slight
bump the mortars make
as they kiss the tubes good-bye.
Then the furious rain,
a fist driving home a message:
"Boy, you don't belong here."
On good nights they walk them in.
You wait for them to fall,
stomach pinned so tight to ground
you might feel a woman's foot
pace a kitchen floor in Brownsville;
the hushed fall of a man lost
in a corn field in Michigan;
a young girl's finger trace
a lover's name on a beach along Cape Cod.
But then the air is sucked
straight up off the jungle
floor and the entire weight
of Jupiter and her moons
presses down on the back of a knee.
In a moment, it's over.
But it takes a lifetime to recover,
let out the last breath
you took as you dove.
This is why you'll see them sometimes,
in malls, men and women off in corners:
the ways they stare through the windows in silence.

Prodigies

During the worst of those days,
they packed up the children
and sent them to the country.
The gifted ones went first.
The soldiers came, loaded pianos,
piles of instruments, moved
them in a single day fifty miles
north of the capital, past
guns, green searchlights,
to foothills, old factories
where the children lived and studied
the next four years.

Weekends, the children
charted elaborate escapes,
stole over compound walls,
joined the lines that thronged
the roads at night,
returning to the capital.

You could pick them out
if you looked closely,
the way they tensed and leaned;
as if it took all their strength
to hold up the sky.

Temple at Quan Loi, 1969

Outside the gate
the old woman
walks up the hill
from the temple.
Her pace
deliberate as a procession.
From the corner of an eye
she stares.
She must wish our deaths.
Beneath the white silk band
breasts ache for a husband.
She passes in mourning,
counting each step.
Her prayers rain down like rockets.

Pictures of the Buddha

At Wat Po a thousand Buddhas stare.
Through half-opened eyes and outstretched hands
they seem to call —
you too could be at peace.

So many forms happiness takes.
Sunday's, eyes are open.
Monday's, standing, hand out against calamities.
Tuesday's is reclining, brings clemency.
Wednesday's, alms bowl held at waist.
Thursday's, meditation. Friday, contemplation.
Saturday, under the Naga hood.

In the courtyard teenage students
from The Fashion School seem less
in love with this than with each other.
Behind their teacher's back, they steal touches.
Young children from the temple school
file by and giggle.

Beneath his canopy outside,
a young monk smokes and listens.

President Diem's Motorcade

President Diem's limousine
turns up Le Loi
away from the river.
The passers-by all know
the President's Peugeot,
can tell by the stern profile
the President
is reassuring the Ambassador
once again
of his great concern for the peasants.
Two hours now
since the President took communion.
The car rocks just a bit;
the President turns,
wonders, all the monks in the streets,
then something he'd meant
to ask in confession.

Willie, Dancing

When we moved south
we found comfort
nights at base in new dug bunkers,
the womb hum of generators,
artillery thud and mortars
marking time. And whiskey,

always whiskey and hot music
you had sent from home —
Louisiana blues.
In the cool night, we smoked opium,
danced in bare dark soles
in the red clay dust,
making promises for home.

But here it begins to fade.
I don't remember you leaving us
or hearing they'd saved you
after all that shrapnel
lifted you from the ground.

Still, as I sit here sipping whiskey
late at night
I see you dance
in trails of smoke above my head.

Banded Kraits

Blackburn saw him first,
called us over
just as he poked his head up,
four of us
hovering over the hole
at the bottom of the slumped pile
of sandbags
at the old French base camp.
He lingered a second,
then quick as it took
to take our measure,
squirmed back down,
flipping his tail at us
as if in some obscene gesture.
But already the gasoline
was on its way. Morales
held the five-gallon can
carefully over the hole
as we watched to see
if the snake would crawl out again
as gas sifted into dirt
and the thin slit in the earth
that was his home
disappeared and reappeared
in slow migrations of sand
that seemed the pulse
of somebody's heart
we couldn't remember
until Morales dropped a match
and the blaze slunk down
the hole after.

He came out slowly.
One good shot
straight through the head
put him away.
We laid him out,
all four feet of him and fangs.
Enough time to smoke a cigarette
was what he'd give you.
The same that we gave him.
Then, babies, someone said.
We smoked and joked
our way to the green line.
Cambodia, the rains, June's weeping light.

Graves at Quảng Trị

Troung Son Cemetery, Quảng Trị, January, 1987

Too late, tanks circle the old French tower
on the hill above the square.
They rust in a silence only snakes invade.
On the turret of one, a red poster
announces a dance tonight.

I know a man who stood here once,
and wounded, pledged
before moon, wind, and sky
to take back his home
in seven more days.
The next day he rolled
into the capital.

My friend Hao was there,
with the starving ARVNs
behind the church.
They passed rat meat at ends of stakes
from hole to hole.
The fire so heavy, he says,
he still wears it like a shirt.

Yesterday, in the old capital,
a young girl in white au dai
led me through a dark schoolhouse,
her face lit faded monochromes
of heroes hung on walls.
Outside, three children

broke off and chased me
through fields behind the Citadel.
I taught them English
behind the Palace of Full Peace,
whose name they taught me:
Điện Thai Hoi.

Now your names are on my lips.
Three friends who left the North together,
buried here above Côn Thiên Hill,
Hill of Angels.
What can I say to you?
Peace has come. The land has changed.
But bombs still explode,
rip arms and eyes from farmers.
Fish never returned.
Each year more topsoil washes off.
Spring, the forests lose more cover.
But still the full moon on the hill
restores belief, and nights the young go dancing.
On even rainy days the market's full,
and miles from here, young girls
raise their eyes to heaven,
listen for footsteps,
mouth your names.
Nguyễn Cao Đai, Nguyễn V. Kich, Vũ Đình Cát,
the enemy we stayed.

Núi Bà Đen: Black Virgin Mountain

for Crisp

1

In dreams you've returned before.
Last night, smoking
cigarette after cigarette,
pacing across the room,
ship lights blinking
up and down the Saigon River,
I saw you again
and all the others.

What mouth could speak
that last moment of fear?

2

Highway 13.
The dust penetrates, ages us
inch by inch as it rises
along the road.
In tropic heat, whirlwinds —
taunting brown ghosts —
rise up from the ground,
at every bend
and are gone.

We drive straight into the landscape —
a flat panhandle,
unpeopled, and spare.
A sole shape beckons,

the Black Virgin Mountain:
Núi Bà Đen,
the widow who waits her soldier's return.

3
Standing below the mountain,
I see you here again
after twenty years.
Red hair gleaming in the sun,
faded brown fatigues
stuffed with letters to Miriam
back in Georgia.

What green thoughts
rise in your mind;
what grace is found
in so much loss?

4
Jungle trails
still lead back
up the mountain,
past streams and caves
where children hide.

One last time
I kiss the red dirt
that holds you,
suck in again
your last breath,
return it to the wind
that blows down
Núi Bà Đen, home
at last.

Missing

How you put those dots together and got Beethoven
was a mystery. Third grade nuns didn't teach you that.
Or how it was you were home when the TV host called
so you could yell the answer to your grandmother,
who looked blankly at the screen, not half-believing
the man in there could be the same one on the phone.
Back in Scotland, in the village where she came from,
things didn't happen like that.

You won three Edsels and a trip to Disneyland.
Then in California, on another quiz, you won prizes
for your sister, who was not that sick.
Your parents bought a summer house that year.
We charged your boat across the lake.
Nights, we snuck in back of the Casino,
watched your cousin dance in tight black slacks.
Our world was movies and rollerskates, shooting
bb's at dogs, and taking lessons in sex from the locals.
Mornings, behind the lake we hunted frogs for bait,
stuck our hooks down long green spines
to lure the pickerel. The force of the strike
still wakes me late at night.
What came between us I don't remember,
only getting on the bus, and the call,
my brother sick.

I followed your story after that.
Military school, marriage to an heiress.
Someone said you'd tried to kill yourself,
I doubted it, at least your luck had saved you
until that pilot caught you in his sights

over Ha Long Bay. What did you think
as you fell, the cars, the boats,
the girls, the picture of a boy
on the mantle in kilts?
Whose face did you see
mapped across the sky?
I was there that day, felt the tug,
looked down and saw my own face
looking up to me from the paddy,
searching the sky where already you'd disappeared.

Thiên Quang Lake

Beneath the window, the street sweeper
makes his slow morning pass around the lake.
Lights of the V.I.P. Club
burn amber in trees by the guest house
where the power has just returned,
the fan lifting the thick night air.

On a long journey I have woken
many times in the night
dreaming of the ones I love.

Deep in the dark of the room,
I turned to find them in postures
I know best. One kissed me deep
on the throat. One clapped
from a bed. One opened a door to my room.

What I didn't know was how far
we take the ones we love
into our bodies, how deep
we carry them until they call out
on nights like this, on a lake
whose name is the Buddha's Light.

The Arts of Love and Hydrology
as Practiced in Hà Nội
for Thuy

During the monsoon
in the North she digs
a hole outside
the stucco complex
where she shares
a nine-square-meter flat
with her father, mother,
and younger brother.
In the mornings at five,
she rises from her
hammock and begins
her chores before leaving
for the ministry.
Last, she dips the jars
of smoky glass down
into a fetid pool,
sets them by the hearth
then takes the route
she always has,
past the old school and canal.

It seems so distant now
that day she dove and dove
for him. She'd been
among the first pulled
back from the canal,
the bombs still falling.
They couldn't understand her
as she gestured

back to the water.
Then she left them, dove back in,
found him, drew him
up the bank where she pumped
the brackish waters
from her brother's chest.
Some of the children trampled,
she later learned, rushing from road
and school into the flooded ditch.

Still, evenings she returns
the same way; arriving home
again she checks to see
if the clay has settled
in the jars so she can cook.
Some nights the hues of crimson
in the rice will trouble
her as she lies in her
hammock dreaming late
of a lover laying
fresh-water pipe across
the broad green
fields of the delta.

Body Count: The Dead at Tay Ninh

We had no place to put them
so we piled them, boots
pointed to the sky,
by the mess tent.

All day they kept coming.
I saw one man run from a swirl of dust,
and sit beside them, and his look
when he realized where he was.

By afternoon, the sick and lame
who'd missed the ships
came to gaze in disbelief.
Bodies so close together lies came easy.
They slept; they weren't really dead.
They'd wake up when the war was over.
This was it for them.

Dusk, the last ones came from the Angel Plain;
the grass had caught on fire.
Their bodies black and crisp curled in the purple light.
Dawn, we flew them out in bags,
mopped up the mess for chow.

Banking Lesson, 1970

Your hero's welcome was cleaning
floors at the local bank
for minimum wage.
A little joke to start the day,
leaning on a pole, a train
rumbling through a tunnel,
a blue janitor's uniform from Sears
replacing olive green.
You were reading Stendhal,
stuck in your back pocket like a confession.
Each day, seven a.m., you began your tour
sweeping tape across the computer room,
everyone watching, you could tell.
Knock first before checking
the washrooms for paper stock,
empty trash pails for executives.
If they knew the murder in your head....
Lunch was a cafeteria filled
with girls in six-inch heels
and men in blue suits.
You ached as you passed through the line.
Back by the loading docks
you smoked your wrath up,
watched armored trucks bring
the day's deposits from the branches.
How far could you get, you wondered,
Wednesdays mopping the main vault,
stacks of bills rising in piles on the walls.
How far?

At the Tomb of Tự Đức

He was a man of tangled inclinations,
never chose to run the empire.
Each morning, the tiger and the dragon
would have been enough. Or long walks
down white-flowered paths,
bright pavilions
built above the River of Perfumes.
In all desire he was an addict.
Each dawn his wives set out
in sculpted boats
to pick dew from lotus cups for tea.
At dusk in his theater,
girls from mountain tribes
cooled his cheeks with camphor,
players acted out his verses
beneath a jewel and timber sky.
Drunk on such nectars
he kept a hundred wives.
All those slender rowers
and never a child.

Playing Basketball with the Viet Cong

for Nguyễn Quang Sáng

You never thought it would come to this,
that afternoon in the war
when you leaned so hard into the controls
you almost became part of the landscape:
just you, the old man, old woman
and their buffalo.
You never thought then
that this grey-haired man in sandals
smoking Gauloises on your back porch,
drinking your beer, his rough cough
punctuating tales of how he fooled
the French in '54,
would arrive at your back door
to call you out to shoot some baskets, friend.
If at first he seems awkward,
before long he's got it down.
His left leg lifts from the ground,
his arms arch back then forward
from the waist to release the ball
arcing to the hoop, one, two,...
ten straight times. You stare at him
in his tee shirt, sandals, and shorts.
Yes, he smiles. It's a gift,
good for bringing gunships down
as he did in the Delta
and in other places where, he whispers,
there may be other scores to settle.

Peasant Fare: Meditations on
a Museum Catalogue Found in
the Bến Thành Market, July 1988.

Why in these paintings of the Middle Ages
are the peasants so plump and healthy,
always posed in inns and taverns
drinking, grabbing loaves of bread
in dark, knotted hands, hands
stained with blood and large with work?
The men and women seem to drown in conversation,
nod with lustful eyes,
or plot as they brush away
gobs of beef that hang
above their open mouths.
Off to the side, sits
the mandatory dwarf or giant,
playing with the children.
It's as if the painter
thought the peasants' life
only a homelier version of the nobles',
that the bounty of the good old days
spread to plain and simple
folk who made it.
More likely, the painter
was well paid for his subterfuge.
By the age of ten
half we know were dead;
the rest, beaten and worked to stupor.
The women raped and sold
on a regular basis,
and a whole science of torture for doubters.
All this missing from these paintings.

Only far off in a corner
a look of treason beneath a cap,
or in green eyes, a hint of truth,
the pure and honest terror.

Gelatin Factory

No need to look for the place,
just follow your nose,
the man at unemployment
said, not sure he was joking.
Down where the river turned
and the factory rose,
there were always jobs
on the night shift.
Only you and the foreman
would know English.
Not Héctor and José,
who punched in late
those summer nights
from bars still cursing
women, baseball and the Colombians.
Maybe it was nostalgia
for the heat that brought them.
Never less than 100 degrees
on the catwalks, more near
the ovens. And all summer
men of many colors dying
in jungles and cities of Asia.
But only pigs died here.
You didn't believe at first,
but then you saw the evidence:
morning, freight cars,
loaded like ships to the gunnels
with carcasses of dead piglets,
pulled onto the sidings.
All day, their small, twisted bodies
grayed in the sun, legs

pointed to the heavens
that failed them.
No farmer to claim
the honor of this crop,
raised to be boiled in acid,
rendered a sticky mass
rolled on screens and cooked
in sheets to glass, smashed
and ground to a fine powder
useful for many things
but best for those sweet desserts,
late on Sundays, children
circled and ate.

In the Village of Yen So

After the dust of the village brick factory,
she offers tea,
bitter green oranges for respite.

Numbers tumble in our heads:
how many commune members
comprise how many families

sharing how many hectares of land
producing how many tons of rice,
fish, maize, bricks, carpets,

piglets, and yes, children,
like the boy who peers in
at the door.

In silence we scribble facts
into notebooks. Nguyễn Thị Chu,
quietly moves about the tables

serving tea, her mind fixed on other numbers.
Fifteen years ago. Christmas Day. The guns,
the arcing lights, then rush of flares.

Two hundred fifty-eight killed that night.
Five hundred who went south to war.
Two hundred and sixteen who didn't return.

She remembers the names, the eyes,
wishes we could see them
as she does, staring in at the door.

Pictures from Quảng Nam

for Leslie, Đà Nẵng 1989

The picture brings it back.
You and Mrs. Mai.
You walk side by side,
bodies almost touching,
stare to a distance
I still can't fathom.

Beneath the gray pocked wall
outside the orphanage, the camera
has caught the image of four women,
backs bent, carrying nuts to market.
Their baskets hang on tips of bamboo poles,
sweep the road bed.

From our balcony over the square
you watched the light die on the mountains,
shadows fall over villages below.
You turned back to the room
to the vase on the table
and counted twelve purple flowers.

It was hard to sleep in the heat,
the two beds separating us for the first time.
You woke many times, finally
to see him laying across my bed,
a soldier, you said, a figure in black,
arm draped across my shoulder
as if to protect me.

You tried not to think. Only in this city
could it happen. You knew that already,
didn't panic or scream, slipped
back into the darkness. In the morning,
you counted the flowers, knowing
one would be gone.

Lotus Tea

for Vũ Tú Nam

Last night in Hà Nội.
Outside the V.I.P. Club,
cabs line up.
Bright orange lamps
light the entrance.
Three nights have passed
and now the first men
and women push past
the cyclo drivers and prostitutes
by the park.

Jammed into a narrow
restaurant booth, his large
hands open, he shows
how the leaves are placed just so
in lotus petals at night,
then plucked again,
dew scooped out,
when flowers bloom in morning.

Tonight, Lotus tea.
Tomorrow, Children's Tet.
How to say good-bye.
My wife's grandfather's grave
is in Huế, he whispers,
buried next to Phan Bội Châu.
His face disappears in the tea like a river.

The Children's Tet

Crowds so thick on Trần Hưng Đạo
they pass bicycles over their heads
to get close to the student troupe
acting the old story.
The figure in black unmasked,
the dragon slain, fireworks
light the river,
traffic moves again.
Tonight the children rule.
In torch-lit packs
hunch-backed dragons
snake down streets,
chasing drums follow.
Who is head or tail
will change as they charge
into shops straight up
into the world of their elders.
Parents watch, not yet sure to be afraid.
One boy's eyes search the crowd,
he beats his chest in confusion,
but has no need for worry,
tonight the city is filled with dragons.

A Conical Hat

for Lê Cao Đài and Vũ Giáng Hương

A moment of awkwardness
as he bends to lift the gift
to the table, not as if
he could hide it, the broad
conical shape of the *"non la"*
stared up at us all through dinner,
the girl who served us
stepping around it
as if to draw attention all the more.

Across the table all night
I watch the stories
come alive in his eyes;
I can almost see the bulb burning;
a man pedals a bicycle underground,
in the shadows of the bunker
he makes power for lights and suction
in the operating room.
Lungs burn, he inhales
fine red bits of earth.
They are digging to expand the tunnels,
make more room for the wounded.

A figure in white
draws a suture through
last bits of skin,
prays his sight holds.

One day he walks
straight off the earth,
right into the brown, wrinkled
hide of an elephant,
carves meat for a starving platoon,
takes machete and scalpel,
makes cut after cut
until he's covered
in blood and muscle,
fighting for air.

1970. A break in the fighting.
A game of volleyball, interrupted.
A gunship sprays the pitch.
Two nurses killed, he drags
their bodies down, heavy
and smoking, into the tunnels.

Ten years, his wife
slept in mountain caves,
after bombs, repaired roads,
made posters, paintings
to record each detail.

"Ham Rong Bridge, 1970, " he shows me.
A woodcut on rice paper.
Two women in conical hats
load rocks along a road.

In the background trucks
grow wings of camouflage,
rattle across the bridge
heading south.

His eyes burn as he looks
through the woodcut.
I thank him. I will need this hat,
the cool circle of its shade.

The Temple of Literature

Hà Nội, 1987

Nine hundred years they traveled,
new students seeking fame,
fresh from village lanes to enter
in ceremony here,
the gate on the right, the Gate of Virtue.
Then after years of study,
mastering lu-shih, lục bát,
to march at last through the northern gate,
the Gate of Success.
At night though did they whisper
the privilege and wonder of mandarins,
who alone could pass the middle throne
and circle in peace
the Well of the Quiet Heart?

The Tây So'n Armies

When the Tây So'n soldiers
whooped through the countryside
swearing and hissing,
goading even the skies
with their jibes,
the people said
the sounds they made
were the rage of waves
breaking night after night
over the dikes; their voices,
the cries of tigers
flaying the moon
in the dust.
And evenings they slept,
people said, they rose
in the morning,
a field of white cranes
stretching their wings
from mountains to coast.

The Quiet Americans

for Tô Nhuận Vỹ

We hold our glasses out,
then drink.
Two years since the American soldier returned,
told how he'd turned his claymores
facing up that night: so the warning,
"This side to the enemy,"
pointed to the sky.
His one small act of protest in the war.

He never knew at midnight, a troop of artists
had passed along the dike, suspected,
one day, one of them would sit beside him
listening as he told the story,
suddenly remember stumbling
on the mines
aimed strangely at the heavens.

There were photos and embraces.
But two years now and not a letter
from the soldier.
He can't understand it. I nod
"How could a man who did such a thing forget?"
We turn back to the young singers,
the sad and lovely music.

Chung's House: The Liberation of Hà Nội

This is one way the war ends.
Six men sit shirtless on the floor,
top floor of a triple decker
in Somerville, Mass.
The air smells of asphalt and tar.
Under a bright August moon
murder is done
in record numbers this summer.

Across the interstate headed north,
we stare into the dull yellow brick
of the projects where the shots sounded.
Canada, three hundred miles.
How many fled the war this way?

Below, cars pass, unaware the enemy
is poised above the road.
All night we talk, wait, pass rations
back and forth, cigarettes and beer,
cups of sweet coffee, stories
of what we've done, the war,
and of one dark woman from Cuba
who taught with her tongue
impossible things.

Song in the Green Light

For Hà Khánh Linh

A young girl sings in the green light,
songs of leaves on the river, evening rain.
She strains to keep time with the boy
who fights the feedback of his bass.
Her voice, so clear, holds the strength
of her song high out over the audience.
Men, women, and children who've come to the hall
drawn by the songs piped over loudspeakers.
In rumpled shirt and tie, her teacher
stands nervously to the side. Now the boy
at his feet changes the spotlight
from green to red, exposes a cracked
plaster wall, paintings by children.
Boats drift on black rivers,
villages hang suspended under October moons.
The sadness of autumn gathers here.
I remember your words.
"Hope is an unharvested field."

Midnight, The Cửu Long

The top floor, Saigon's grand hotel,
my wife lies stretched across the emperor
Bảo Đại's mistress's bed, asleep
beneath the creaking fan.

All night I toss and turn.
Spirits rise from the river.
They come, sleepwalkers,
thin mustached men bearing
cocktails to women in au dais
who bend over pianos and great carved chairs
to laugh at the general's newest joke
about the president.

From walls, legends watch,
spun by craftsman's art,
inlaid in mother of pearl,
the Trưng sisters and Trần Hừng Đạo.

River Music

One by one the lanterns
swim off down river.
A green one first, then red
and yellow. Each one calls
back a friend. Like dancers
they turn in circles.
One for my wife, one for my son,
one for our new child in spring.
Back and forth they swing
in twos and threes, seeking
ever newer combinations.
We drink rice liquor, toast
ten reasons men fall
in love on a river.
The old men smile into their instruments.
A woman sings, such beauty
even the moon might die
on her shoulder.

Reunion

for Lê Trí Dũng

Forty years. Too long a separation.
She paces a white stucco kitchen
in a house as far south
as you can get in Louisiana,
remembers the day of their parting,
how they packed the altar on the cart,
walked the lonely roads south, 1956,
the first year of their trials.
Now she weaves through open rooms
waits for her guest to follow.
She must prepare the old dishes
for the stranger, the young man
who has come to recite
the ancient words of greeting.
Religion and politics are cruel brothers,
but sisters must always be true.
Yes, she tells him, she prayed for him,
her sister's son, driving his tank from Hà Tây,
thought of him often, pictured him under the bombs.
But she never thought they would meet like this,
that she would be the one to leave,
he, the first to cross the threshold to her kitchen.
All night, like figures in his paintings,
they reach for sun and moon on wings,
ride above a plain of sorrow.
She places lemongrass, shrimp paste, sticky rice,
fresh and steaming before him.
The war closes its circle around them.

The Snail Gatherers of Cổ Loa Thành

The legends of Cổ Loa Thành, Old Snail City,
tell how spirits of Mount Tam Đảo
tried to stall the citadel
by slipping down the hills each night
to undo the labor of the day.
One night a golden
tortoise crawled up river,
gave the king new weapons, bows
to slay the spirits of Tam Đảo.
And so the city rose
carved from carcasses and shells.

Tonight, from old city walls strange shapes
rise on the night and wind
down old trails.
Some bear lights in hand;
others on their heads like miners.
From the balcony of the guest house
I hear their voices call.
How have they gotten past the guards,
breached the compound walls and lake?

At every tree, shadows pause.
Some move on hands and knees,
examining each blade of grass.
And why not? What gems
compare with these: the snails of Cổ Loa,
and their gatherers back again.

And we without our bows.

"Beautiful....Bowen captures the spirituality of Vietnam."
—Oliver Stone

"In his invaluable poetry, Kevin Bowen takes us through our war in Vietnam. He tells the terrible and awful truth of it. Reading these poems gives us the understanding and compassion to end that war and come home."
—Maxine Hong Kingston

"It is a beautiful book, one I'll always treasure."
—Tim O'Brien
author of *Going After Cacciato*

"Take this book into a quiet place...Let these poems go like sunlight to your heart."
—Larry Heinemann
author of *Paco's Story*

"This is a different kind of 'Vietnam' book; this collection evolves around a natural empathy between actors on a human stage that's almost mythic in scope and concerns...This poetry is shaped out of a love for people, as well as a painful passion garnered from the experience of war. One feels that a witness is sharing heartfelt moments when reading."
—Yusef Komunyakaa
1994 Pulitzer Prize for Poetry

Kevin Bowen served in the Vietnam war during 1968-69. He is currently Co-Director of the William Joiner Center for the Study of War and Social Consequences at the University of Massachusetts-Boston.

CURBSTONE PRESS

1-880684-20-9   CONTEMPORARY POETS SERIES $10.95

ISBN 1-880684-20-9
51095>
9 781880 684207
EAN